Bedřich Smetana

Má Vlast

No. 2: Vltava (Die Moldau)

Edited by / Herausgegeben von
Milan Pospíšil

EULENBURG

Contents / Inhalt

EAS 142
ISBN 978-3-7957-6542-2
ISMN M-2002-2366-8

© 2007 Ernst Eulenburg & Co GmbH, Mainz
for Europe excluding the British Isles
Ernst Eulenburg Ltd, London
for all other countries
Edition based on Eulenburg Study Score ETP 472
CD ℗ 1994 & © 2001 Naxos Rights International Ltd

Ernst Eulenburg Ltd
48 Great Marlborough Street
London W1F 7BB

Preface

Composed: 19 November – 8 December 1874
First performance: 4 April 1875, Žofín Hall, Prague, Czech Opera
Orchestra, conductor: Adolf Čech
First publication: F. A. Urbánek, December 1879 (piano duet arrangement);
1881 (full score)
Instrumentation: piccolo, 2 flutes, 2 oboes, 2 clarinets; 2 bassoons –
4 horns, 2 trumpets, 3 trombones, tuba – timpani – percussion (triangle,
bass drum, cymbals) – harp – strings
Duration: ca. 13 minutes

There are few among those of the most popular symphonic poems in the repertoire that speak with such a poetic clarity and descriptive precision as Smetana's *Vltava*. The germination of the work has been ascribed to the occasion of a visit Smetana had made on 28 August 1867 to the confluence of the river's two sources at which the composer observed its seasonally shifting appearance with the focus of an Impressionist painter. The work is also to a great extent a summation, since it is a unified expression of the social duty Smetana felt, in that role, to his country and a personal gesture in the face of tragic circumstances. Almost at the same time that he began formulating the work, the debilitating symptoms of syphilis took hold of him during 1874, in the form of permanent deafness accompanied by raging tinnitus which obscured all hope of hearing any music ever again.

Despite this, and with perhaps a Beethovenian defiance in retaliation against his sudden deafness, Smetana began work on his series of symphonic poems – of which *Vltava* is the second in the sequence – to which eventually he gave the simple but powerful title *Má Vlast*, 'My Country'. Although they can often be found programmed separately, the present work undoubtedly most of all, Smetana intended them to be heard as a single 'multi-movement' work. The cycle is a descriptive symphony in all but name. Originally planned as a four-work cycle, to be called *Vlast*, 'The Fatherland', the work would have proved even closer to this conception.

The Vltava, or Moldau river, is central to the Bohemian consciousness in terms of its symbolism and codification of a national cultural ideology. Geographically, it is the longest river in what is now the Czech Republic, flowing the best part of three-hundred miles, and emptying eventually into the Elbe. There is a two-fold narrative unfolding in Smetana's symphonic poem: one that traces the physical path of the river, from the bubbling up of the incipient stream at its two sources through to the broad grandeur of an estuary – that full range of landscape drama being clearly evident in the progress of the musical gestures; the second aspect is the appearance, growth and flowering of a nation – this a more symbolic thread – suggested not simply by the scenes of hunting and village weddings but also by the profession of proud patriotism at the extended coda. This hymn-like pride evident in *Vltava* can be found in the more dedicated exposition of nationalism in *Blaník*.

The introductory section, 'First source of the Vltava', that precedes the clear, folk-like theme at letter A is – next to Debussy's *La Mer* – perhaps the most exquisite depiction of the natural movement of water in the orchestral literature. Eddies swirl and spiral across nearly 40 bars of flutes and clarinets centred closely around the note E almost throughout. The broad, E minor melody, whose long sweep in violins and oboes immediately conjures a great river in the mind's eye ensues; the rippling waters drive on in the lower strings. The river painted thus with obvious clarity, Smetana's patriotic narrative thread is first evinced by the woodland hunting scene that immediately follows.

At bars 80–117, 'Forests – Hunting', we are clearly no longer being carried along by the undaunted currents of the Moldau. Smetana's adoption of the river more as 'some great mighty thought threading a dream' – a symbol for life's or a national continuum, is shown in the bugle calls and equestrian vaunting in the strings. This leads to the 'Village Wedding' at bars 118–176 and the metre changes to an almost May-song, four-square 2/4 contour. The river is a backdrop and a bloodline that connects the composer on an individual level to his nation's past but similarly connects the listener to a universal expression of social unity through a shared cultural heritage.

The section at bars 181–238, 'Moonlight – Dances of water-nymphs', is a hauntingly sensitive paragraph of orchestral colours. Three layers are melded together here: the agitated water's surface in flutes and clarinets, embraced by a tranquil halo of muted, divided strings; the distant brass fanfares that emerge from held chords offer a mysterious background urgency.

The river meanders back to the foreground at bar 239 – a musically structural recapitulation of the main theme at letter A that leads us smoothly but deceptively to the abrupt cataract of the St John Rapids at bars 271–332. As the river broadens at the *Più moto* in bar 333, we are led inexorably back to the Bohemian age of heroes and *Vyšehrad* – a rocky outcrop of historical and mythological importance near Prague – the first piece in the cycle, whose theme appears here at the close of *Vltava*.

David Lewiston Sharpe

V

Vorwort

Komponiert: 19. November – 8. Dezember 1874
Uraufführung: 4. April 1875, Žofín-Palast, Tschechisches Opernorchester,
Leitung: Adolf Čech
Erstveröffentlichung: Urbánek, Dezember 1879 (Bearbeitung für Klavier
zu vier Händen); 1881 (Dirigierpartitur)
Besetzung: Piccoloflöte, 2 Querflöten, 2 Oboen, 2 Klarinetten in C;
2 Fagotte – 4 Hörner in C, 2 Trompeten in C, 3 Posaunen, Tuba – Pauken –
Schlagwerk (Triangel, große Trommel, Becken) – Streicher
Dauer: ca. 12 Minuten

Nur wenige der bekanntesten Sinfonischen Dichtungen sprechen mit solch einer poetischen
Klarheit und anschaulichen Genauigkeit, wie es bei Smetanas *Moldau* der Fall ist. Die Ent-
stehung des Werkes wird auf einen Ausflug zum Zusammenfluss der beiden Quellen der
Moldau zurückgeführt, den Smetana am 28. August 1867 unternommen hatte und bei dem
der Komponist das jahreszeitlich geprägte Erscheinungsbild des Flusses mit den Augen eines
impressionistischen Malers wahrgenommen hatte. Das Werk drückt eine gesellschaftliche
Verpflichtung aus, die Smetana seinem Land gegenüber empfand, ist zugleich aber auch eine
persönliche Geste angesichts der tragischen Umstände. Fast zur gleichen Zeit, als er mit der
Konzeption des Werkes begonnen hatte – im Laufe des Jahres 1874 – zeigten sich die ihn
schwächenden Symptome der Syphilis in Form von dauerhafter und mit heftigem Ohren-
sausen einhergehender Taubheit. Dies ließ jede Hoffnung Smetanas schwinden, jemals wie-
der Musik hören zu können.

Trotz allem, und vielleicht mit einer Beethovenschen Rebellion als eine Art Vergeltung für
seine plötzliche Taubheit, begann Smetana die Arbeit an seiner Serie Sinfonischer Dichtungen, von denen *Die Moldau* die zweite ist. Er gab der Serie schließlich den einfachen, aber
ausdrucksvollen Titel *Mein Vaterland*. Auch wenn die einzelnen Teile oft separat aufgeführt
werden – vor allem der vorliegende –, hatte Smetana sie eigentlich als ein einziges mehr-
sätziges Werk vorgesehen. Der Zyklus kann de facto als eine programmatische Sinfonie
bezeichnet werden. Ursprünglich als ein viersätziger Zyklus mit dem Titel *Vlast* („Vaterland")
geplant, hätte das Werk noch besser zu dieser Konzeption gepasst.

Die „Vltava" oder Moldau ist mit ihrer symbolischen Bedeutung hinsichtlich einer nationalen
und kulturellen Ideologie ein wesentlicher Bestandteil des böhmischen Bewusstseins. Geo-
grafisch betrachtet ist die Moldau der längste Fluss der heutigen Tschechischen Republik. Sie
ist rund 440 Kilometer lang, fließt zum größten Teil durch dieses Land und mündet schließ-

lich in die Elbe. In Smetanas Sinfonischer Dichtung finden sich zwei Erzählungen: Auf der einen Seite wird der tatsächliche Weg der Flusses vom ersten Herausprudeln der beiden Quellen bis hin zur breiten Flussmündung beschrieben. Dabei zeigt sich deutlich die ganze Breite der Landschaft in der Entwicklung des musikalischen Ausdrucks. Auf der anderen Seite stehen die Entwicklung und das Aufblühen eines Volkes. Dieser mehr symbolische Handlungsstrang wird nicht nur durch die Jagdszenen und Bauernhochzeiten angedeutet, sondern auch durch die Bekundung eines stolzen Patriotismus in der ausgedehnten Coda. Diesem offenkundigen Stolz begegnet man auch in der national geprägten sinfonischen Dichtung *Blaník*.

Die einleitende Passage, „Die Quelle der Moldau", die dem klaren, volksliedähnlichen Thema bei Buchstabe A vorausgeht, ist neben Debussys *La Mer* vielleicht die schönste Darstellung der natürlichen Bewegungen des Wassers in der Orchesterliteratur. Wasserstrudel wirbeln fast 40 Takte lang in den Flöten und Klarinetten herum und winden sich beinahe die ganze Zeit dicht um die Note E. Es folgt eine breite Melodie in e-Moll, deren lange Bewegung in den Violinen und Oboen sofort einen großen Fluss vor dem geistigen Auge erscheinen lässt, während das Geplätscher des Wassers in den tiefen Streichern weitergeht. Der Fluss wird auf diese Weise deutlich und klar beschrieben, und Smetanas patriotischer Handlungsstrang zeigt sich erst in der Jagdszene im Wald, die unmittelbar darauf folgt.

In den Takten 80–117, „Waldjagd", werden wir eindeutig nicht mehr von der starken Strömung der Moldau mitgetragen. Smetanas Einsatz des Flusses als „ein großer, bedeutender Gedanke, der einen Traum einfädelt" ist ein Symbol für das Leben oder eine nationale Kontinuität, was sich durch die Hornsignale und die stolzen Reiter in den Streichern zeigt. Dies führt in den Takten 118–176 schließlich zur „Bauernhochzeit", welche durch einen Wechsel in einen unerschütterlichen 2/4-Takt charakterisiert wird. Der Fluss bildet den Hintergrund, der den Komponisten auf einer persönlichen Ebene mit der Vergangenheit seines Volkes verbindet; aber er vermittelt auch dem Zuhörer den allgemeinen Ausdruck einer gesellschaftlichen Einheit, die durch ein gemeinsames Kulturerbe entstanden ist.

Die Passage in den Takten 181–238, „Mondschein – Nymphenreigen", ist mit seinen orchestralen Klangfarben ein sehr ergreifender und empfindsamer Abschnitt. Drei Ebenen werden hier miteinander kombiniert: die aufgewühlte Wasseroberfläche in den Flöten und Klarinetten, umgeben von einem ruhigen Schein der gedämpften, geteilten Streicher, sowie die entfernten Fanfaren in den Blechbläsern, die aus gehaltenen Akkorden entstehen und einen mysteriösen und eindringlichen Hintergrund bilden.

Der Fluss schlängelt sich in Takt 239 in den Vordergrund zurück. Eine musikalisch strukturierte Reprise des Hauptthemas von Buchstabe A führt uns schließlich zu den schroffen St. Johann-Stromschnellen in den Takten 271–332. Wenn der Fluss in Takt 333 beim *Più moto* breiter wird, werden wir unausweichlich ins böhmische Zeitalter der Helden und nach „Vyšehrad" – ein Ort mit historischer und mythologischer Bedeutung in der Nähe von Prag – zurückversetzt, also in das erste Stück des Zyklus, dessen Thema am Ende der *Moldau* noch einmal erscheint.

David Lewiston Sharpe
Übersetzung: Uta Pastowski

Vltava

(První pramen Vltavy)
(First source of the Vltava)
(Die erste Quelle der Vltava)

Bedřich Smetana
(1824–1884)

EAS 142

© 2007 Ernst Eulenburg Ltd, London
and Ernst Eulenburg & Co GmbH, Mainz

2

(Druhý pramen
(Second source of
(Die zweite Quelle

Vltavy)
the Vltava)
der Vltava)

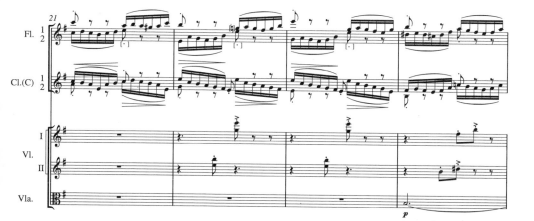

4

EAS 142

10

(Lesy - honba)
(Forests - Hunting)
(Wälder - Jagd)

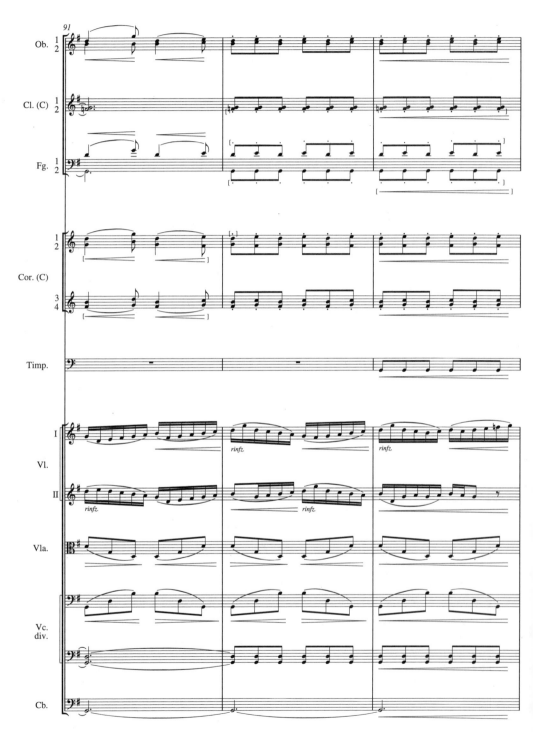

(Venkovská svatba)
(Village wedding)
(Ländliche Hochzeit)

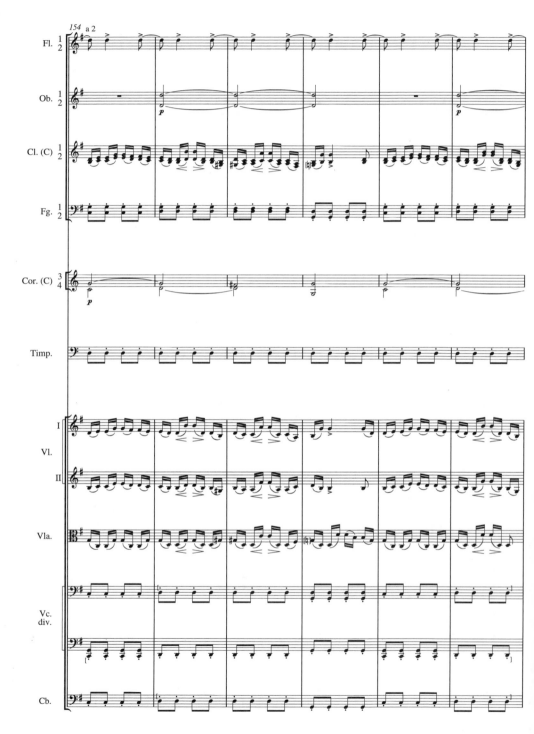

(Luna - rej rusalek)
(Moonlight - Dances of water-nymphs)
(Mondschein - Nymphenreigen)

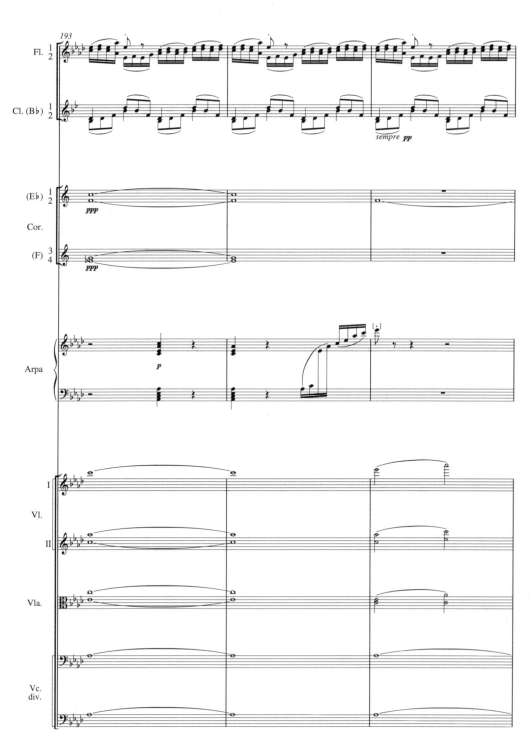

42

44

54

(Svatojanské proudy)
(St John Rapids)
(St. Johann-Stromschnellen)

60

(Široký tok Vltavy)
(Vltava, powerful stream)
(Der breite Strom der Vltava)

EAS 142

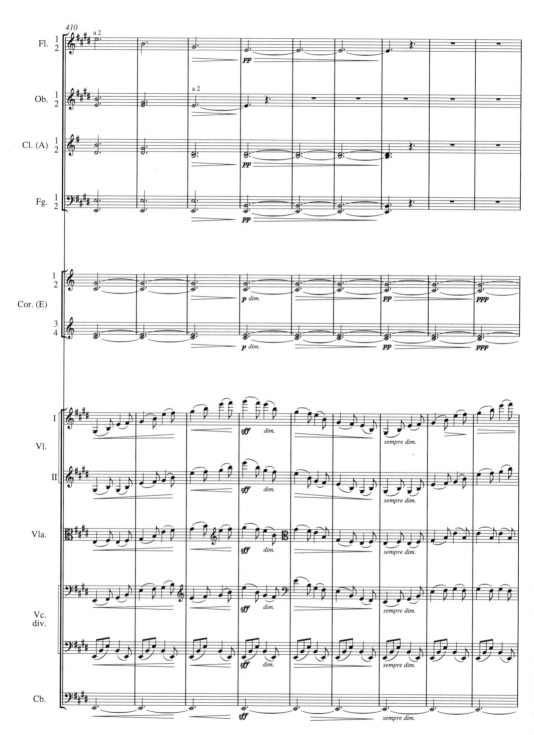

Printed in China